Generously donated by

Mom, Dad and Eamon

in celebration of

Leia Perez's   1ST Birthday

June 14, 2013

WHERE DO YOU LOOK?

By **Marthe Jocelyn**
& Nell Jocelyn

Tundra Books

For Gordon

Text and illustrations copyright © 2013 by Marthe Jocelyn and Nell Jocelyn

Published in Canada by Tundra Books, a division of Random House of Canada Limited, One Toronto Street, Suite 300, Toronto, Ontario M5C 2V6

Published in the United States by Tundra Books of Northern New York, P.O. Box 1030, Plattsburgh, New York 12901

Library of Congress Control Number: 2012934217

Library and Archives Canada Cataloguing in Publication

Jocelyn, Marthe
      Where do you look? / by Marthe Jocelyn and Nell Jocelyn.

ISBN 978-1-77049-376-6. – ISBN 978-1-77049-377-3 (EPUB)

      1. English language – Homonyms – Juvenile literature.
I. Jocelyn , Nell II. Title.

PE1595.J63 2013   j428.1   C2012-901556-3

We acknowledge the financial support of the Government of Canada through the Canada Book Fund and that of the Government of Ontario through the Ontario Media Development Corporation's Ontario Book Initiative. We further acknowledge the support of the Canada Council for the Arts and the Ontario Arts Council for our publishing program.

ONTARIO ARTS COUNCIL
CONSEIL DES ARTS DE L'ONTARIO

Edited by Sue Tate and Samantha Swenson
Designed by Leah Springate
The artwork in this book was rendered in paper collage and mixed media.

www.tundrabooks.com

Printed and bound in China

1 2 3 4 5 6   18 17 16 15 14 13

Where do you look for a **cap**?

On a tube of toothpaste?

Or on your head?

Where do you look for a **button?**

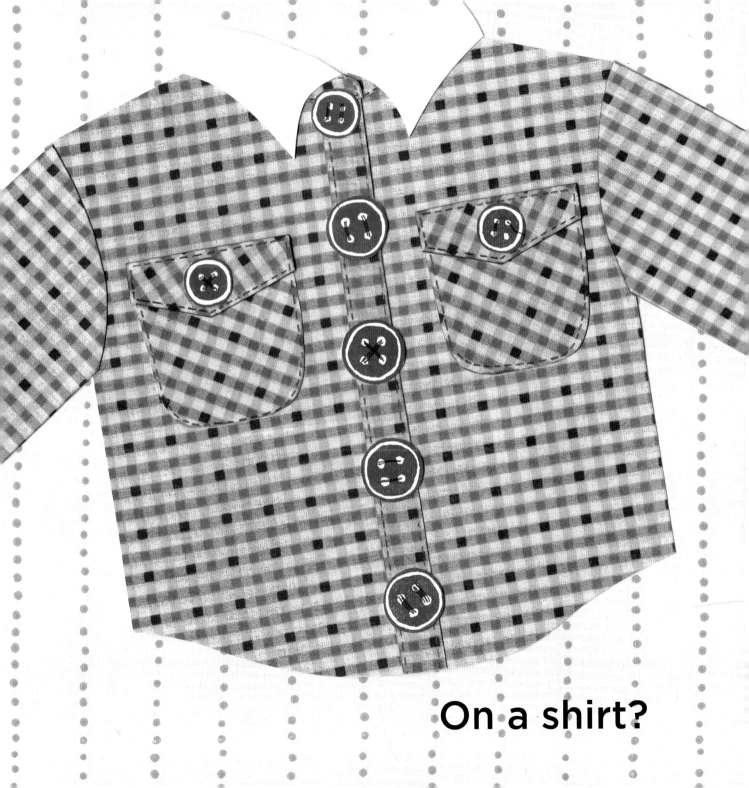

On a shirt?

Or on a telephone?

Where do you look for a **tongue?**

In a shoe?

Or in your mouth?

Where do you look for glasses?

On a shelf?

Or on a face?

Where do you look for a match?

In the laundry?

Or on a soccer field?

Where do you look for a wave?

At the train station?

Or at the beach?

Where do you look for a **trunk?**

In the attic?

In the garden?

Or on your elephant?

Where do you look for a letter?

In the mailbox?

W R O I
K E V M
D B Y Z

Or on the page?

Where do you look for a story?

On a building across the street?

Or in your own bed?